High-Interest/Low-Readability Graphic Novel

Miles and Lizzie Save the Earth

An 8 Chapter High-Interest Graphic Novel
About 13 Year Old Detectives
Miles Masters and Lizzie Blizzard —
Complete with Comprehension Activities and Audio CD

by
Jo Browning-Wroe
and
Sherrill B. Flora

illustrated by
Julie Anderson

Publisher
Key Education Publishing Company, LLC
Minneapolis, Minnesota

CONGRATULATIONS ON YOUR PURCHASE OF A KEY EDUCATION PRODUCT!

The editors at Key Education are former teachers who bring experience, enthusiasm, and quality to each and every product. Thousands of teachers have looked to the staff at Key Education for new and innovative resources to make their work more enjoyable and rewarding. Key Education is committed to developing and publishing educational materials that will assist teachers in building a strong and developmentally appropriate curriculum for young children.

PLAN FOR GREAT TEACHING EXPERIENCES WHEN YOU USE
EDUCATIONAL MATERIALS FROM KEY EDUCATION PUBLISHING COMPANY, LLC

Credits
Authors:.. Sherrill B. Flora and
                                                    Jo Browning-Wroe
Art Director: .... Annette Hollister-Papp
Illustrator: .... Julie Anderson
Editor: .... Karen Sebreg
Production: .... Key Education Staff

Audio CD Voice Talent:
The voice of Miles Masters .... Jeffrey O. Standke
The voice of Lizzie Blizzard .... Kasandra S. Flora
The voice of the Narrator .... Sherrill B. Flora
The voice of Voor .... Timothy M. Irwin
The voice of Urso .... Mike McCullum
The voice of Kate & Person B.......... Kathryn E. Flora
The voice of the Logger,
   Hunter, and Police Officer........... George C. Flora
The voice of Diner Owner .... Keith M. Brings
The voice of the Singer.................... Sherrill B. Flora
The voice of Alien A & Person A..... George C. Flora
The voice of Alien B .... Sherrill B. Flora
The voice of Alien C & Person C .... Keith M. Brings

Key Education welcomes manuscripts and product ideas from teachers. For a copy of our submission guidelines, please send a self-addressed, stamped envelope to:
Key Education Publishing Company, LLC
Acquisitions Department
9601 Newton Avenue South
Minneapolis, Minnesota 55431

About the Author of the Stories:
Jo Browning Wroe has taught both in the United Kingdom and in the United States. She earned her undergraduate degrees in English and Education from Cambridge University, Cambridge, England. She worked for twelve years in educational publishing before completing a Masters Degree in Creative Writing from the University of East Anglia, Norwich, England. Most of her time is now spent writing teacher resource materials and running workshops for others who love to write. Jo has been the recipient of Britain's National Toy Libraries Award and a Teacher's Choice Award. She lives in Cambridge, England with her two daughters, Alice and Ruby, and her husband, John. This is Key Education's seventh book written by Jo Browning Wroe.

About the Author of the Activities:
Sherrill B. Flora is the Publisher of Key Education. Sherrill earned her undergraduate degrees in Special Education and Child Psychology from Augustana College and a Masters Degree in Educational Administration from Nova University. Sherrill spent ten years as a special education teacher in the inner city of Minneapolis before beginning her twenty-year career in educational publishing. Sherrill has authored over 100 teacher resource books, as well as hundreds of other educational games and classroom teaching aids. She has been the recipient of three Director's Choice Awards, three Parent's Choice Awards, and four Teacher's Choice Awards. She lives in Minneapolis, Minnesota with her two daughters, Katie and Kassie, and her very supportive husband, George.

Standard Book Number: 978-1-602680-07-4
High-Interest/Low Readability:
Miles and Lizzie Save the Earth
Copyright © 2008 by Key Education Publishing Company, LLC
Minneapolis, Minnesota 55431

Introduction

About the Graphic Novel

All of the chapters and activities found in *High Interest/Low Readability Graphic Novel: Miles and Lizzie Save the Earth* have been specifically designed for students who are reading below grade level; for students who have reading disabilities; and for students who are reluctant or discouraged readers.

The engaging chapters are written between the early first grade through mid-second grade reading levels. Each chapter's specific reading level and word count can be found above the chapter title on the Table of Contents (page 4). This information will help guide the teacher in choosing chapters that are appropriate for the individual needs of the students. *(Reading grade levels are not printed on any of the chapters or on any of the reproducible activity pages.)*

Since struggling readers are often intimidated and easily overwhelmed by small print, each chapter was created with an easy-to-read font. The font, picture clues, and sentence structure will help the children feel more self-confident as they read the chapters included in *High Interest/Low Readability Graphic Novel: Miles and Lizzie Save the Earth*

All of the stories use high-frequency words and essential vocabulary. A list of the story's high-frequency words, as well as any special words that are necessary for each chapter, are found on pages 60 and 61. Prior to reading each chapter, review the word lists and introduce and practice any unfamiliar words. Discuss the meaning of each new word. Make flash cards of the new words and outline each letter with glitter glue to provide a tactile experience for the students. Draw a picture of the word on each card to help the students visualize any new vocabulary.

About the Audio CD: "Miles and Lizzie Save the Earth"

Each chapter comes with its own auditory narration — read by the story characters — and begins with a few seconds of introductory music. Following the music, the narrator will provide the number and title of the chapter. That is the student's clue to listen. The story characters will then read the content of the chapter exactly as it is printed on the student's copy.

For many struggling readers, being able to listen to each chapter first can be extremely beneficial. Knowing the content ahead of time provides students with the opportunity of using context clues to help decode words and for interpreting the meaning of the story. For other students, being able to track the text as they listen to the words allows for a multi-sensory experience. Students can hear the words; see the words; and can touch each word as they follow along while listening to each of Miles' and Lizzie's exciting adventures.

About the Activity Pages

Paper and pencil tasks are often "not fun" for struggling readers. The majority of the reproducible activity pages are divided into two different activities per page. The teacher may choose to assign both halves at once. The diversity of the two different activities should encourage the children to finish the page and not become bored or frustrated. The teacher may also choose to cut the page in two and assign each half at different times.

Coloring, drawing, solving puzzles, and cutting and pasting activities have been included. These types of activities reinforce a wide range of reading skills and are often viewed as "more fun" by the students.

In short, *High Interest/Low Readability Graphic Novel: Miles and Lizzie Save the Earth* will provide your students with a complete reading experience.

Contents

Miles and Lizzie Save the Earth

Chapter 1 - The Future

Narrative: From the age of 4, Lizzie Blizzard knew how to travel back in time. She liked to meet people from the past. They told her their stories. When she got back, she wrote them down. On April 10, 1980, Lizzie turned 13 years old. Also on this day, she found out that she could time travel — into the future! The future scares her. The forests have been cut down. There are very few animals. The oceans have no fish. The Earth is one big landfill.

Can Lizzie change history? Can she find out what's happened? Lizzie needs help and she knows just who to ask, Miles Masters. He is the one friend who knows that Lizzie can time travel. He's not a superhero, but he is the smartest person Lizzie knows.

1. Miles, I need you to come to the future with me.

Are you kidding? I'm scared of heights! I get sick! You need a superhero — not me!

2. Please come with me, just once. You can figure out what's going on.

Ok. Just this once.

3. Here we go! Hold tight. Don't look down.

Too late! Aaaaaaah!

4. Where has all this trash come from? Where are all the trees?

I don't know. Hold on.

5. Are you sure this is Earth?

Yes. This is the future — unless you agree to help me.

6. Why didn't anyone stop this from happening? We've got to find out.

I knew you'd help.

Narrative: Miles tells Lizzie that they need to go to the end of time. If there's someone or something that wants to kill the planet, they'll be there at the end. Lizzie is scared to go so far ahead in time. It takes all her powers, but she does it. They circle the empty Earth. Finally, they spot some people. The people are cheering and clapping.

But . . . are they human people?

End Chapter 1

Name ______________________________

Complete Sentences

Directions: Choose the correct word from the Word Bank to complete each sentence.

Word Bank:	heights	Lizzie	help	Thet	Miles	planet	1980

1. ______________________ Blizzard can time travel.
2. Lizzie asks __________________ for help.
3. Miles says, "Yes, I will ____________________ you."
4. Miles is scared of ___________________ .
5. Miles and Lizzie see a destroyed ________________________ .
6. Aliens from planet _____________________ have come to Earth.
7. Miles and Lizzie live in the year ___________________.

Inference

Directions: Pretend you are Miles Masters or Lizzie Blizzard.
Draw and color a picture of what you think planet Thet looks like.

Name _____

Directions: Read the sentences at the bottom of the page.
Cut them out along the dotted lines and glue each sentence under its matching picture.

Lizzie and Miles fly
into the future.

Aliens have taken
over the Earth.

The oceans have no fish.

The forests have
been cut down.

Chapter 2 – Superpower Surprise for Miles

Narrative: Miles asks Lizzie to take him to a library in the year 2000. He is amazed to find out about the internet. He reads that each year, more than one billion trees are used to make diapers. In just one minute, 50 acres of rainforest can be chopped down. Next, Miles and Lizzie are going to time travel ten years into the future and visit a rainforest.

Turn the page.

Turn the page.

Narrative: Lizzie thinks they should go back home. Miles now thinks they have to fight Voor. They must tell people that Voor's ideas are killing the planet. Miles wants to try one more time to talk to the man.

End Chapter 2

Name _____

Directions: Read each sentence about the story. Write a "**T**" on the blank if the sentence is true. Write an "**F**" on the blank if the sentence is false.

1. The rainforest is home to animals, plants, and insects. _____

2. The man could see and talk to Voor. _____

3. In one minute, 50 acres of rainforest can be chopped down. _____

4. In 20 years there will be enough dirty diapers to reach the moon. _____

5. Voor grabbed Lizzie's arm. _____

6. Miles has superpower arms. _____

Directions: Draw a line from the sentence (**Column A**) to the person who said that sentence (**Column B**).

<u>Column A</u>	<u>Column B</u>
1. "This isn't over. You won't stop us!"	a. Lizzie
2. "Hi. It's me. I've had an idea. Diapers! We're going to be rich! Diapers are going to make us rich!"	b. Miles
3. "Miles, what did you do?"	c. Voor
4. "I don't know. Something flew out of my arm."	d. Man in the rainforest

Name _____

Directions: Circle the words from the Word Bank in the word search. The words may be horizontal or vertical.

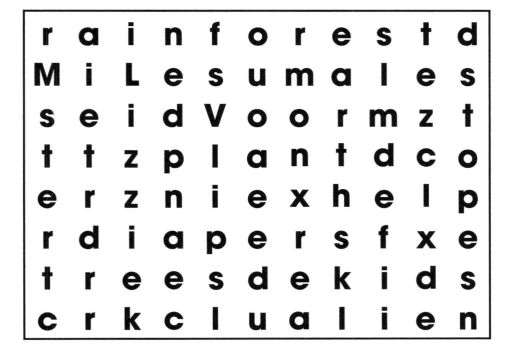

r a i n f o r e s t d
M i L e s u m a l e s
s e i d V o o r m z t
t t z p l a n t d c o
e r z n i e x h e l p
r d i a p e r s f x e
t r e e s d e k i d s
c r k c l u a l i e n

Word Bank

help
plant
Lizzie
Miles
rainforest
earth
Voor
trees
diapers
alien
kids
stop

Drawing Conclusions

Directions: Miles discovered that he has a superpower. Do you think Miles has any other superpowers? Write your thoughts.

_____

- -

_____

- -

_____

- -

_____

- -

_____

- -

_____

Miles and Lizzie Save the Earth

Chapter 3 — Pop in the Park

Narrative: Miles and Lizzie go forward in time. They find out about internet cafes. They spend hours finding out about the future. Miles learns why the planet is in danger. He finds out how bad cars are for the environment. Miles has an idea. Each Sunday, his family goes to the park. There's always a band playing and everyone brings a picnic lunch. All the people love the park. They love nature!

Turn the page.

Turn the page.

Narrative: Lizzie and Miles watch Voor. No one can hear him. Miles thinks that once humans hear the truth, they will no longer be able to hear Voor. Miles and Lizzie get up and start walking away from the bandstand. They are ready to go home.

End Chapter 3

Name _____

Directions: Unscramble the sentences. Add the correct punctuation marks.

1. are   doing   What   they

   _____

   -

   _____

2. did   How   that   do   you

   _____

   -

   _____

3. going   again   to   sick   I'm   be

   _____

   -

   _____

Cause and Effect

Directions: A **cause** tells why something has happened and an **effect** tells what happened. Draw a line from each cause in **Column A** to its matching effect in **Column B**.

Column A

1. Each time you drive a car,

2. Miles gets sick,

3. Traveling through time,

4. Miles and Lizzie saw what could happen to the Earth,

Column B

a. makes Lizzie tired.

b. because they were able to time-travel into the future.

c. when he travels through time.

d. you put bad stuff in the air.

Directions: Read the question in each box. Write your answer in each speech bubble.

1. What could Miles be saying to Lizzie?

2. What could the singer be saying to all the people?

3. What do you think Voor is saying to the other Thetan?

4. What could Miles be saying to Voor?

Chapter 4 - Voor Talks with Lizzie

Narrative: Miles and Lizzie spend more time in the future at the internet cafe. They find out what's going to happen to the planet. And it doesn't sound good!

Turn the page.

Narrative: Lizzie and Miles walk through the forest. They see gorilla's playing together. The babies are on the backs of their mothers.

Turn the page.

Narrative: Lizzie and Miles run away, fast! The kids are scared. Lizzie tells Miles to hold on as they time travel to get away. They land in the rain forest again, but they must have gone forward in time. Much of the forest is gone. There are loggers cutting down the trees. They see Voor whispering to a man.

Turn the page.

Name _____

Directions: Read each sentence about the story. Write a "**T**" on the blank if the sentence is true. Write an "**F**" on the blank if the sentence is false.

1. Male gorillas are called "silverbacks." _____

2. In this chapter. the loggers take money from the poachers. _____

3. In this chapter, the loggers plant trees. _____

4. Voor "zaps" Miles and makes him fall asleep. _____

5. Voor talks to Lizzie and tries to get her to come over to his side. _____

6. Voor wants to eat a hamburger. _____

Drawing Conclusions

Directions: Miles fell asleep. Voor talks to Lizzie alone. Write about if you think Lizzie will help, or not help, Voor.

_____

_____

_____

_____

_____

_____

Name _____

Directions: Choose a word from the Word Bank to answer each crossword clue. Write the answers in the correct word boxes.

ACROSS

3. Lizzie and Miles traveled to a _____.

5. Miles and Lizzie want to put an _____ to Voor's plans.

6. Time travel makes _____ sick.

Word Bank
rainforest end
Miles Voor
save time

DOWN

1. The evil alien is named _____ .

2. Lizzie and Miles can _____ travel.

4. Miles and Lizzie want to _____ the Earth.

Directions: **Antonyms** are two different words that have opposite meanings. For example, "hot" and "cold" are antonyms. Draw a line from each word in **Column A** to its matching antonym in **Column B**.

Column A

save

girl

happy

scared

fast

forward

Column B

brave

slow

destroy

backward

boy

sad

Chapter 5 — Saved by the Leopards

Narrative: Back home, Lizzie is not herself. She doesn't want to save the Earth. She doesn't want to time travel. She just wants to eat fast food. It's driving Miles crazy.

Turn the page.

Narrative: Miles went on a walk — alone — just to think. He knows that Voor got to Lizzie. He tries to figure out how he can get Lizzie back. Miles comes up with a plan. He has to get Lizzie to time travel again.

Turn the page.

Narrative: Miles and Lizzie spent time in the library in the year 2020. When they were at the library they learned that snow leopards were extinct. Finally, for the first time since the kids have returned, Miles sees the old Lizzie. Lizzie wipes a tear from her eye, and then she gets angry with Miles.

Turn the page.

Turn the page.

End Chapter 5

Name _____

Directions: Circle **yes** or **no** for each sentence.

1. Miles got a big bump on his head.   **yes**   **no**

2. Miles got the bump when he tripped.   **yes**   **no**

3. Miles wants Lizzie to see some snow leopards.   **yes**   **no**

4. The poachers came to hunt the snow leopards.   **yes**   **no**

5. Voor is trying to save the Earth.   **yes**   **no**

6. Lizzie and Miles saved the lives of 3 cubs.   **yes**   **no**

Directions: Circle the words from the Word Bank in the word search.
The words may be horizontal or vertical.

s	n	o	w	l	e	o	p	a	r	d
a	s	t	i	a	a	i	n	g	e	i
h	a	M	b	u	r	g	e	r	k	e
o	h	i	z	g	t	e	f	o	o	l
m	o	l	g	h	h	s	c	a	r	e
e	o	e	o	m	w	o	u	f	x	z
s	l	s	r	p	w	i	b	n	e	o
p	o	a	c	h	e	r	s	u	k	o

Word Bank
snow
leopard
earth
poachers
hamburger
Miles
zoo
cubs
care
laugh
fool
home

Name _____

Directions: Look at the pictures at the bottom of the page.
Cut them out along the dotted lines and glue them in the correct order.

1	2
3	4

Miles and Lizzie Save the Earth

Chapter 6 — On Planet Thet

Narrative: Back home Lizzie is very upset. Miles and Lizzie need to come up with a plan to save all the animals that might soon become extinct. That will not be easy.

Turn the page.

Narrative: Back on planet Thet, there is a big meeting of the Thetan Council. Every 30 days Voor returns home to the planet Thet. He reports how his team is doing to the Thetan leader Urso and the Council.

Turn the page.

Turn the page.

Narrative: While Voor is on Planet Thet, Lizzie and Miles go back in time and travel around the world. They go and visit all the animals that will soon become extinct.

Pandas live in China and eat bamboo.

19.

The Bengali tigers in Nepal are beautiful!

20.

The elephants in India help people.

21.

Look at the strong black rhinos here in Kenya.

22.

Orangutans in Malaysia are so much fun to watch.

23.

The Bottlenose dolphins are swimming off the coast of Scotland.

24.

Turn the page.

Turn the page.

Narrative: Miles tells Lizzie his idea, and she has to admit, it's a good one. They travel back to their own time. The kids are tired and hungry from all their travels, so they go to their favorite diner. At the diner, they plan how they are going to put Miles' plan into action.

Turn the page.

Narrative: Kate is excited about the idea and promises to write to the WAF about it. Miles and Lizzie give her the list of animals that they know are in danger from their trips to the future. Kate wants to know where they got the list. Miles says he found it in a cafe that has computers. Kate thinks that sounds like a crazy kind of cafe, but she takes the list. As Miles and Lizzie walk home, they don't notice they are being followed.

End Chapter 6

Name _____

Directions: A **fact** is something that is true. An **opinion** is something that a person thinks, believes, or feels. Write the word "**fact**" or the word "**opinion**" next to each sentence.

_____ 1. Voor tells Urso that Lizzie and Miles can time travel.

_____ 2. Voor and Urso are very clever.

_____ 3. Elephants are beautiful animals.

_____ 4. Animal habitats are being destroyed.

_____ 5. Kate is a member of the World Animal Fund.

Creative Writing

Directions: Pretend you are a member of the World Animal Fund (WAF). What two questions would you ask Miles and Lizzie?

_____

- -

_____

- -

_____

- -

_____

- -

Name _____

Directions: Design a poster about becoming a member of the World Animal Fund.

Cloze

Directions: Choose the correct word from the Word Bank to complete each sentence.

Word Bank:	baby	Animal	paper	Urso	days	trees	Voor

1. The leader of the Thet Council is _____.

2. Voor must report every 30 _____ to the Thet Council.

3. Just one human _____ can use 6,000 diapers in two years.

4. Four billion _____ are cut down each year to make

   _____.

5. Kate is a member of the World _____ Fund.

6. Miles and Lizzie finally believe that _____ will lose.

Chapter 7 — Urso's Order

Narrative: On planet Thet, Urso has called another meeting of the Council.

Turn the page.

Turn the page.

Turn the page.

Narrative: Back at home Lizzie and Miles are excited. They are pleased about the WAF's "Adopt-an-Animal" idea. Trees are being planted every day. More people are using public transportation. Now, Miles has a new idea. He is telling Lizzie all about it.

Turn the page.

Narrative: Miles and Lizzie suggest why and how everyone should recycle. Next, they visit companies that make paper, glass, and plastic. Miles and Lizzie ask them to think about making things from recycled materials. At last they travel home. They are tired and hungry and need to eat.

Turn the page.

Narrative: Miles and Lizzie are worried that Voor has been looking for them. And, they should be worried. The Thetan Council has been told that Urso has given Voor two days to get rid of Miles and Lizzie.

Turn the page.

Narrative: They tie Kate's hands and put her in the back of a car. Kate kicks and shouts, but the Thetans ignore her and drive out of the city. At last, Voor turns around.

Panel 43:
- Kate: "Where are you taking me? Let me out!"
- "Why do humans make such a fuss?"

Panel 44:
- "You humans? What are *you* then? Aliens?"

Panel 45:
- "Shall we give her something to shout about?"
- "Why not?"

Panel 46:
- "Oh, really?"
- Kate: "You don't scare me."

Panel 47:
- "AAAAAAAAAAAH!"

Panel 48:
- "It's what they call fainting. At least we'll get some peace and quiet."
- "Has she fallen asleep?"

43. 44. 45. 46. 47. 48.

End Chapter 7

Name _____

Directions: Read the sentences at the bottom of the page.
Cut them out along the dotted lines and glue each sentence under its matching picture.

1.

2.

3.

4.

Lizzie and Miles are
at the diner.

Voor is going to take
Kate away.

Urso is talking to Voor.

Voor is talking
to the Thetans.

Name _____

Directions: Choose a word from the Word Bank to answer each crossword clue. Write the answers in the correct word boxes.

Word Bank: Thet   Earth   environment   plan   planet   Voor

DOWN
1. We live on planet_____ .
2. _____ is an evil alien.
3. Voor is from planet _____.
4. Miles and Lizzie have a _____.

ACROSS
1. Take care of the _____.
5. Earth is a _____ .

Directions: Read the word boxes at the bottom of the page. Which words describe Lizzie? Which words describe Miles? Which words can be used to describe both of the children? Cut out the word boxes along the dotted lines and glue them into the correct section of the Venn diagram.

Lizzie

both children

Miles

| has a superpower finger | loves animals | girl |
| boy | wants to save the Earth | can time travel alone |

Miles and Lizzie Save the Earth

Chapter 8 — Good-Bye Voor

Narrative: Lizzie and Miles are in the diner having a soda. They want to talk to Kate and find out how the WAF's plans are going. But, Kate's not at the diner. Where could she be?

Turn the page.

Narrative: Lizzie and Miles are in shock after Voor hangs up the phone. They don't know what to do. They have to rescue Kate, but if they do, the planet will die. Miles suggests they go to the police.

Turn the page.

Narrative: The next morning Miles knocks on Lizzie's door. They agree to go to the diner. Miles suggests that when Voor calls, they should say they need to see Kate alive before they will talk with him.

Turn the page.

Narrative: Lizzie and Miles are driven for miles, out into the country. They arrive at an old warehouse. The building is full of aliens.

Turn the page.

Turn the page.

Turn the page.

Turn the page.

Narrative: When the new school year begins, Miles and Lizzie arrive at school with a stack of papers. At recess they give them to all their friends and teachers. They stick them on all the doors, walls, and lockers. The Principal reads one and smiles. She tells Miles and Lizzie that they are ahead of their time. I can't tell you what Miles told the police, because he still hasn't told Lizzie, but I can tell you what it said on the papers that the kids hung all over their school.

TAKE CARE OF OUR PLANET

1. Turn off lights, TVs, music systems, and radios when not in use.

2. Unplug cell phone chargers when not in use.

3. Turn off the faucet when you brush your teeth.

4. Take reusable bags to the grocery store.

5. Use recycled paper and then recycle it again.

6. Take the bus, subway, ride a bike, or walk.

7. Don't buy things made at the expense of the rainforest.

8. Do buy things that come from the rainforest.

9. Plant trees.

10. Adopt an endangered animal.

11. Get all your friends to do all of the above.

World Wildlife Federation offers a range of animal adoptions from anacondas to zebras: www.worldwildlife.org

Asia Animals Foundation has an adapt a moon bear program: www.animalsasia.org

Whale and Dolphin Conservation Society and adopt a whale: www.wdcs.org.uk

Wildfowl and Wetlands Trust offers ducks, geese and swans for adoption: www.wwt.org.uk

Care for the Wild offers a range of animal adoptions from tigers to badgers: www.careforthewild.org

| End Chapter 8 |

Cause and Effect

Directions: A **cause** tells why something has happened and an **effect** tells what happened. Draw a line from each cause in **Column A** to its matching effect in **Column B**.

Column A

1. Cutting down the rainforest,

2. Turning off the faucet while you brush your teeth,

3. Adopting an endangered animal could,

4. Buying recyled paper and recycling used paper,

Column B

a. can help save the forests.

b. takes away the homes of many animals.

c. will conserve our water resources.

d. help save that species of animal.

Comprehension

Directions: Read each question. Circle the picture that answers each question.

1. Who did Voor take?

3. Who has a superpower finger?

2. Who was the leader of the Thet Council?

4. Who did Miles go to for help?

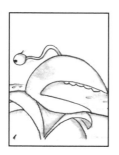  

Name _____

Direction: What do you think Miles told the police?

_____

- -

_____

_____

- -

_____

Direction: Write what you think happened to Voor when he returned home.

- -

_____

_____

- -

_____

Directions: Circle **yes** or **no** for each sentence.

1. Voor took Kate and put her in a plane.   **yes**   **no**

2. Lizzie called Kate and she answered the phone.   **yes**   **no**

3. Voor did not want to hurt Miles and Lizzie.   **yes**   **no**

4. Lizzie knew that Miles went to the police station. **yes**   **no**

5. Lizzie and Miles lost their superpowers.   **yes**   **no**

6. Voor went back to planet Thet.   **yes**   **no**

High-Frequency, Easy-to-Sound Out, and Special Words for Each Story

a	before	come	fallen	good	invent	market	out
able	begin	could	families	got	is	math	outside
about	behind	cub/s	family	graze	isn't	maybe	over
action	being	cut	far	great	it	me	own
admit	believe	cute	fast	grow	it's	mean	paper
after	best	cutting	faster	gun/s	just	meant	park
again	better	danger	fastest	guys	keep	meet	past
against	big	day	favorite	had	kept	meeting	peace
age	bit	dead	feel	hadn't	kick	met	people
ahead	blew	deal	feeling	hands	kidding	might	people's
air	book	did	felt	hangs	kid/s	mile/s	person
all	both	didn't	few	happened	kill	mine	phone
almost	brain	died	figure	happy	killed	minute	photo
alone	bravo	diner	film	hard	killing	money	picnics
along	break	dirty	film-maker	has	kind	moon	picture
also	bring/s	do	finally	hat	kittens	more	piece
always	brought	does	find	hate	knew	morning	pills
am	boy	doesn't	finding	have	knock	mother/s	place
amazed	building	dog	fine	haven't	know/s	mouth	plan
an	bump	doing	finger	hear	knowing	much	plant
and	burger	done	first	he/s	landfill	must	playing
angry	bush	don't	fish	he'll	last	my	please
animal/s	bus	donuts	flew	help	late	name	pocket
any	but	door/s	fly	helped	later	nasty	pooling
anymore	by	down	follow	her	laugh	near	poor
anyone	bye	drag	fool/s	here	laughing	neck	pop
April	call/s	drink	for	hero	learned	need/s	pretty
are	came	drive	forest/s	hike	leave	never	problem
aren't	can	driven	forget	him	left	new	promise
arm	can't	each	forgot	his	let	next	power/s
around	care	easier	forward	hold	lets	nice	pulled
as	catch	easy	found	home	life	no	put
ask/s	chance	eat	four	hooray	like/s	noise	quick
asked	change	eaten	friend	hope	list	normal	quiet
asleep	cheering	else	from	hours	listen	not	rains
at	children	empty	front	house	little	nothing	reach
away	chill	end	full	how	live	now	read/s
awful	choice	enjoy	fun	hungry	longer	oceans	ready
babies	choose	enough	funny	hurt	look	of	really
back	chose	even	fuss	hurting	lots	off	remember
bad	chopped	ever	get	I	love	office	return
banana	circle	every	gift	idea	lovely	old	reuse
band/s	clapping	everyone	girl	if	lucky	on	rich
bars	close	evil	give	I'll	lunch	once	ride/s
be	closed	exactly	given	I'm	mad	one/s	right
beat	closer	eye	glass	in	make	only	room
beautiful	clue	face	go	insects	making	or	sad
because	coats	fail	going	inside	man	ouch	safe
been	code	failed	gone	into	many	our	said

saved
say/s
saying
scares
school
scream
see
share
she
shock
shoot
shout/s
show
sick
sickness
sight
silly
sing
singer
sit
six
smart
smartest
so
soda
some
someone
something
song
soon
sorry
space
spend
spoke
sport
spot
stairs
stand
start
stop
stories
stuck
stuff
sure
such
suggest
surprise
Sunday
take
talk

talking
teach
ten
tell/s
than
thanks
that
the
their
them
themselves
then
there
there's
these
they
they'd
they'll
they're
tight
time
thing
think
thinking
tired
this
those
thought
trash
travel/s
through
throw
time
to
today
together
told
tomorrow
too
toys
tree/s
trick
tried
true
trust
truth
try
turn
turned
two

unless
up
upset
us
use
used
uses
very
visit
wait
waiting
walk
walking
want/s
warm
was
watch
way
we
we'd
week
weird
well
we'll
went
were
we're
we've
what
what's
when
where
while
white
who
why
wild
will
win
wire
wish
with
without
wonder
won't
wood
word
work
worked
world

worry
worse
worth
would
wrote
yea
years
yes
you
you'd
you'll
your
you're
yourselves
zap
zapped
zoo

Special Words for Each Story

Special Words for Chapter 1
Earth
energy
future
history
Lizzie Blizzard
Miles Masters
planet
pollute
superhero
Thet
Thetans

Special Words for Chapter 2
alien
billion
biodegrade
dangerous
diapers
environment
internet
library
medicines
rainforest

Special Words for Chapter 3
bandstand
crowd/s
music
nature
project
troubles

Special Words for Chapter 4
Asia
cafe
cattle
elephants
extinct
freeze
gentle
gorillas
graze
hamburgers
hunters
loggers
pandas
poachers
Silverbacks
tigers
whales

Special Words for Chapter 5
film
film-maker
human/s
returned
snow leopard
tomorrow

Special Words for Chapter 6
adopt
badge
brilliant
chocolate
clever
council
destroying

dolphins
genius
milkshake
police
orangutan
organization
report
research
Urso

Special Words for Chapter 7
angry
car-pooling
decide
fainting
guards
hundreds
orders
plastic
programs
public
recycle
recycled
secret
serious
state's
transportation
weapons

Special Words for Chapter 8
arrive
abducted
country
crazy
greedy
police
research
rescue
warehouse

Answer Key

Top of page 7

1. Lizzie;   2. Miles;   3. help;   4. heights;
5. planet   6. Thet;   7. 1980

Bottom of page 7

Check students' work

Page 8

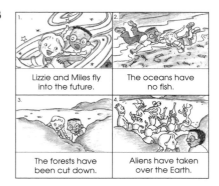

Lizzie and Miles fly into the future.	The oceans have no fish.
The forests have been cut down.	Aliens have taken over the Earth.

Top of page 12

1. T;   2. F;   3. T;   4. T;   5. F ;   6. T

Bottom of page 12

1. c;   2. d;   3. a;   4. b;

Top of page 13

```
r a i n f o r e s t d
M i L e s u m a l e s
s e i d V o o r m z t
t t z p l a n t d c o
e r z n i e x h e l p
r d i a p e r s f x e
t r e e s d e k i d s
c r k c l u a l i e n
```

Top of page 17

1.   What are they doing?.
2.   How did you do that?
3.   I'm going to be sick again.

Bottom of page 17

1. d;   2. c;   3. a;   4. b;

Page 18

Check students' work

Top of page 23

1. T;   2. T;   3. F;   4. T;   5. T;   6. F

Bottom of page 23

Check students' work

Top of page 24

```
        V
    t   o
r a i n f o r e s t
    m   r   a
    e n d   v
        M i l e s
```

Bottom of page 24

save — brave
girl — slow
happy — destroy
scared — backward
fast — boy
forward — sad

Top of page 30

1. yes;   2. no;   3. yes;   4. yes;   5. no ;   6. yes

Bottom of page 30

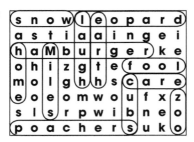

```
s n o w l e o p a r d
a s t i a a i n g e i
h a M b u r g e r k e
o h i z g t e f o o l
m o l g h h s c a r e
e o e o m w o u f x z
s l s r p w i b n e o
p o a c h e r s u k o
```

Page 31

Top of page 39

1. fact;   2. opinion;   3. opinion;   4. fact;   5. fact

Bottom of page 39

Check students' work

Top of page 40

Check students' work

Bottom of page 40

1. Urso;   2. days;   3. baby;   4. trees, paper;
5. Animal   6. Voor

Page 48

Voor is talking to the Thetans.	Urso is talking to Voor.
Lizzie and Miles are at the diner.	Voor is going to take Kate away.

Top of page 49

```
e n v i r o n m e n t
a   o             h
r   o       p     e
t   r     p l a n e t
h         a
          n
```

Bottom of page 49

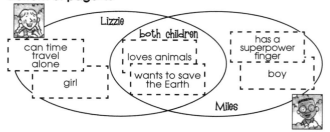

Lizzie

both children

can time travel alone

loves animals

has a superpower finger

wants to save the Earth

girl

boy

Miles

Answer Key

Top of page 58

1. b; 2. c; 3. d; 4. a

Bottom of page 58

1. picture of Kate; 2. picture of Urso;
3. picture of Miles; 4. picture of police officer

Top of page 59

Check students' work

Bottom of page 59

1. no; 2. no; 3. yes; 4. no; 5. yes ; 6. yes

Standards Correlation for
High-Interest/Low Readability Graphic Novel: *Miles and Lizzie Save the Earth*

This book supports the NCTE/IRA Standards for the English Language Arts and the National Science Education Standards.

NCTE/IRA Standards for the English Language Arts

Each activity in this book supports one or more of the following standards:

1. **Students read many different types of print and nonprint texts for a variety of purposes.** *Miles and Lizzie Save the Earth* is a graphic novel, which requires students to read both words and pictures, along with an audio recording of the novel to build both reading and listening skills.

2. **Students use a variety of strategies to build meaning while reading.** Comprehension activities focusing on drawing conclusions, sequencing, inference, reading for details, context clues, cause and effect, fact and opinion, and vocabulary, among other skills, support this standard.

3. **Students communicate in spoken, written, and visual form, for a variety of purposes and a variety of audiences.** Activities in *Miles and Lizzie Save the Earth* incorporate drawing and writing for a variety of purposes.

4. **Students use the writing process to write for different purposes and different audiences.** *Miles and Lizzie Save the Earth* includes creative and expository writing activities focused on a variety of audiences and purposes.

5. **Students incorporate knowledge of language conventions such as grammar, spelling, and punctuation; media techniques; and genre to create and discuss a variety of print and nonprint texts.** Writing activities in *Miles and Lizzie Save the Earth* take different forms, from words to sentences to paragraphs, allowing students to practice different forms of writing and writing conventions.

6. **Students use spoken, written, and visual language for their own purposes, such as to learn, for enjoyment, or to share information.** The engaging story and images in *Miles and Lizzie Save the Earth* will motivate students to read independently and the skill-building activities will support students in becoming more effective independent readers and writers.

National Science Education Standards

This book and the activities in it support the following Science as Inquiry standard for Grades K–4:

1. **All students should develop understanding of what scientific inquiry is.** Throughout *Miles and Lizzie Save the Earth,* Miles Masters and Lizzie Blizzard participate in scientific inquiry, helping readers enhance their own understanding of it.

This book and the activities in it support the following Life Science standards for Grades K–4:
1. **All students should understand the characteristics of organisms.** While reading *Miles and Lizzie Save the Earth,* students learn about organisms such as human beings and gorillas, among others.

2. **All students should understand the relationship of organisms and environments.** Because *Miles and Lizzie Save the Earth* is about saving the earth's environment, the book supports this standard very well.

This book and the activities in it support the following Earth and Space Science standard for Grades K–4:
1. **All students should understand concepts related to changes in earth and sky.** The story told in *Miles and Lizzie Save the Earth* focuses on changes to the earth's environment, so it strongly supports this standard.

This book and the activities in it support the following Science in Personal and Social Perspectives standards for Grades K–4:
1. **All students should develop understanding of concepts related to characteristics and changes in populations.** *Miles and Lizzie Save the Earth* discusses changes in animal and plant populations as related to human actions.

2. **All students should develop understanding of different types of resources.** This book discusses the many resources of the earth and how human actions affect those resources.

3. **All students should develop understanding of concepts related to changes in environments.** *Miles and Lizzie Save the Earth* discusses the changes in the earth's environment due to human actions.

4. **All students should develop understanding of science and technology as they relate to local challenges.** *Miles and Lizzie Save the Earth* helps students realize how science and technology affect changes in their own world.

This book and the activities in it support the following Science as Inquiry standard for Grades 5–8:
1. **All students should develop understanding of what scientific inquiry is.** Throughout *Miles and Lizzie Save the Earth,* Miles Masters and Lizzie Blizzard participate in scientific inquiry, helping readers enhance their own understanding of it.

This book and the activities in it support the following Life Science standard for Grades 5–8:
1. **All students should understand populations and ecosystems.** *Miles and Lizzie Save the Earth* includes information on a variety of earth populations and ecosystems, supporting this standard.

This book and the activities in it support the following Science in Personal and Social Perspectives standards for Grades 5–8:
1. **All students should develop understanding of populations, resources, and environments.** *Miles and Lizzie Save the Earth* discusses changes in animal and plant populations and environments as they relate to human uses of resources.

2. **All students should develop understanding of risks and benefits.** *Miles and Lizzie Save the Earth* presents both the risks and benefits inherent in how people use natural resources.

3. **All students should develop understanding of science and technology in society.** *Miles and Lizzie Save the Earth* helps students realize how science and technology affect society and the earth.